Mountain Biking

Paul Mason

PowerKiDS
press.

New York

Published in 2011 by The Rosen Publishing Group Inc.
29 East 21st Street, New York, NY 10010

First Edition

Senior Editor: Debbie Foy
Designer: Rebecca Painter
Photographer: Michael Wicks
Photoshoot Coordinator: Jon Richards

Library of Congress Cataloging-in-Publication Data

Mason, Paul, 1967-
Mountain biking / by Paul Mason. — 1st ed.
    p. cm. — (Get outdoors)
Includes index.
ISBN 978-1-4488-3296-5 (library binding)
1. Mountain biking—Juvenile literature. I. Title.
GV1056.M372 2011
796.6'3—dc22

2010024154

Photographs:
The author and publisher would like to thank the following people for participating in our photoshoot: Jenny Copnall, Carl Osborne, Jonathan Heard, Rachael Denman, Connor Campbell, Rebecca Pressner, Amy North, Jacob North, Simon North.

All photography by Michael Wicks except
5 bottom Dreamstime.com/Ron Chapple Studios; 24 Dreamstime.com/Jandrie Lombard; 25 top Dreamstime.com/Maxim Petrichuk; 27 image courtesy of Extrawheel (www.extrawheel.com); 28 Dreamstime.com/Ian Turk; 29 Dreamstime.com/Joseph Pankey

Manufactured in China
CPSIA Compliance Information: Batch #WAW1102PK: For Further Information contact Rosen Publishing, New York, New York at 1-800-237-9932

Contents

What is Mountain Biking?

Whatever kind of fun you're after, the world of mountain biking has it by the truckload. From a gentle ride through beautiful countryside to a white-knuckle ride down a rocky slope, mountain biking has something for everyone!

The Dawn of the Mountain Bike

When people first started mountain biking in the 1970s, they used any old bike. Among their favorites were beach cruisers. With thick tires, an upright riding position, and a pedal-backward **coaster brake**, the bikes were great for skidding around corners!

The riders drove to the top of a local hill in a truck, then rode their bikes down on dirt tracks. Even though the bikes were very different from today, the riders shared the same thrill. It's the thrill of being out in the air, away from the honking, fumy traffic, and whizzing around on a bike.

*A mountain biker heads downhill at **full speed**. The first mountain bikers could only dream about fantastic bikes like this one.*

Both wheels leave the ground, as this rider decides it's easier to fly than to ride.

The Wide World of Mountain Biking

Today, there are lots of different kinds of mountain biking. The main two are downhill riding and cross-country:

• Downhill (or **DH**) mountain biking is just what you'd guess: riding downhill. The routes often have steep drops, jumps, and banked turns, making them exciting and challenging to ride.

Repack Racing

The fastest early downhill routes were sometimes called "repack runs." The bikes had coaster brakes, which were packed with grease to make them work properly. The riders used to brake so hard that the grease melted! At the end of a really good ride, they had to repack the brakes with grease —thus the name.

• Cross-country is often called **XC**. It has a bit of everything, from fast downhill sections to flat trails with beautiful views and—of course—long, uphill runs.

DH and XC aren't the only kinds of mountain biking. There are plenty more:

• Freeriding, a form of XC that involves more aggressive techniques, including jumps, riding along narrow trails with a big drop beside them, and other dangerous maneuvers.

• 4X and dual, which are side-by-side races down specially designed courses.

The first mountain bikes were made out of old beach cruisers like this one. The only shock absorbers were the big balloon tires.

• Long-distance racing or off-road touring, where the riders can be on the trail for days or weeks.

The good news is that you can try most of these without having to buy much specialist equipment. All you really need to get started is a good, strong bike and a helmet.

Getting Started

The most important thing when you start is that you're riding a bike strong enough to go off-road—and it's in good condition. Wearing a helmet is also important. Damaging your head in a fall could be very serious. And that's all the equipment you need!

The Bike

There is no need to rush out and buy a new mountain bike before trying the sport. There are plenty of other ways of getting hold of one:

• Borrow a bike from a friend or relative.

• Rent a bike from a cycle shop or tourist center.

• Your local cycling club may run "taster" sessions where people can try mountain biking.

Wherever the bike comes from, check it over and make sure it's safe before you ride off-road. There is advice on what to look for on pages 10–11.

Team stretch! Warming up before a hard ride will help you to avoid injury.

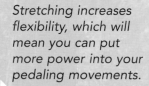

Stretching increases flexibility, which will mean you can put more power into your pedaling movements.

Riding with a group or club is a great way to find out if mountain biking is the right sport for you—before you spend lots of money on a shiny new bike!

Clothes for Riding

The best clothes for mountain biking are light and not too baggy. Wearing layers, rather than one thick top, means you can take clothes off if you get hot. Special cycling shorts and gloves make life more comfortable by providing a bit of padding where your body is in contact with the bike. Finally, stiff-soled shoes make it easier to pedal.

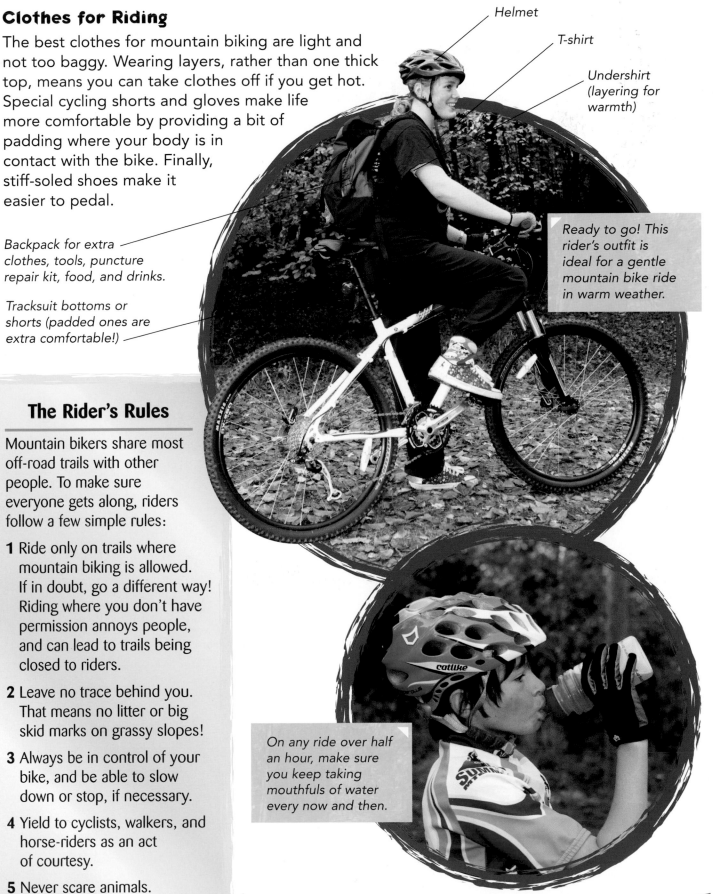

Helmet

T-shirt

Undershirt (layering for warmth)

Backpack for extra clothes, tools, puncture repair kit, food, and drinks.

Tracksuit bottoms or shorts (padded ones are extra comfortable!)

Ready to go! This rider's outfit is ideal for a gentle mountain bike ride in warm weather.

The Rider's Rules

Mountain bikers share most off-road trails with other people. To make sure everyone gets along, riders follow a few simple rules:

1 Ride only on trails where mountain biking is allowed. If in doubt, go a different way! Riding where you don't have permission annoys people, and can lead to trails being closed to riders.

2 Leave no trace behind you. That means no litter or big skid marks on grassy slopes!

3 Always be in control of your bike, and be able to slow down or stop, if necessary.

4 Yield to cyclists, walkers, and horse-riders as an act of courtesy.

5 Never scare animals.

On any ride over half an hour, make sure you keep taking mouthfuls of water every now and then.

Bikes and Bike Set-up

Once bitten by the mountain bike bug, you'll want to get your own bike. Buying new is a big thrill, but there are lots of excellent second-hand bikes around, too. Buying a used bike means you get a lot more for your money. But what kind of bike do you need?

Types of Bike

There is a bewildering range of mountain bikes available. Any specialist bike shop will have a choice of at least these three types:

- Fully rigid bikes
  These are bikes with no **suspension** at the front or rear. Like all mountain bikes, they will have between 18 and 27 gears, and either **rim brakes** or **disc brakes**.

- Hardtail bikes
  A hardtail bike has no suspension at the back, but the **fork** is telescopic. It shortens as you go over bumps and rocks, then lengthen again. This makes for a much smoother ride, and it is a lot easier to hold onto the handlebars on bumpy ground. Hardtails usually have 3–6 in. (80–140 mm) of suspension movement, or **travel**.

A hardtail bike.

Four Steps to Set Up Your Bike to Ride

1 The right size frame

Make sure there is a 1–4 in. (3–10 cm) gap between your crotch and the **top tube**.

2 Saddle angle

Use a spirit level to make sure that the bike's saddle is level with the ground.

3 Saddle height

When you sit on the saddle with your heel on the pedal at its lowest point, your leg should be almost straight.

4 Handlebars

These should be as high as the saddle, or a little higher.

A modern full-suspension cross-country bike. This machine would be able to go just about anywhere.

• Full-suspension bikes
Full-sus bikes have suspension for both wheels. This makes them heavier than hardtails, but more comfortable and easier to ride fast! Most full-sus bikes have 4–6 in. (100–140 mm) travel front and rear.

The rear shock absorber stops too many trail bumps hitting the rider from the back wheel.

Best Bike for a Beginner?

For all-around biking, a lightweight hardtail is the best kind of bike to start with. They are relatively inexpensive, easy to service, and tough. You can also try just about every kind of mountain biking on a hardtail.

Top Tips for Buying a Used Bike

1 Take a friend who is a skilled bike mechanic.

2 Check the bike for faults. Is anything broken? Does it make any funny noises when you pedal it?

3 Check for things that need to be replaced, such as tires or brake pads.

4 Take your time and don't get overexcited because it's the right make, color, or size!

Many modern mountain bikes have disc brakes, which are excellent for slowing you down.

Check Your Bike!

Mountain bikes take some pretty tough punishment. Things can get shaken, knocked loose, or broken. If you don't want to end up with gravel rash or worse, it's important to check your bike before every ride to make sure it's safe. Never set off on a ride knowing that there is a problem with your bike. Always fix it first.

Handling Brakes

- Can you easily reach the levers while holding onto the handlebars? Most brakes are adjustable, and if your hands are small, you can bring the levers closer to the bars.

- Is there space for your fingers between the lever and the bars, when the levers are fully pulled on? If not, the brakes need adjusting.

Quick Releases on Wheels

- Always make sure the quick releases are properly done up. They don't have to be so tight that they are hard to get undone, but it's important you feel some **resistance** when tightening them.

- Make sure the quick releases point backward, otherwise they could get caught on something and be pulled undone.

Wheel Rims and Spokes

- Check that the wheels have not been damaged, by spinning them while holding up the end of the bike. If they are not **true**, you will see a wobble.

Handlebars and Levers

- Check that the handlebars will not move under pressure, by pulling on them while gripping the front wheel between your knees.
- Check that the brake levers and gearshifters are securely clamped to the handlebars.

Tire Pressures

- The best way to check that your tires are pumped up correctly is to use a **pressure gauge**. Most mountain bike tires are designed to work with air pressure of 35–45 psi (pounds per square inch).

Gear Function

- Get a friend to lift the bike's back wheel off the ground, and change gear with one hand while spinning the pedals with the other. Make sure the chain runs smoothly up and down the front and rear gears.

Cranks and Bottom Bracket

- Crouching beside the bike, hold both **cranks** firmly and push them to and fro. There should not be any looseness, or **play**, in them. If there is, the **bottom bracket** may need replacing.

Forks and Headset

- Pull on the brakes, and rock the handlebars forward and backward. There should not be any noises or clicking feeling from the front of the bike. If there is, the forks or **headset** may be loose.

How Derailleurs Changed the Face of Cycling!

Before **derailleurs** were invented in the early 1900s, cyclists could only use one gear at a time. But most bikes only had one gear— a few had two. To change gear, you had to take off the rear wheel and turn it around. Not as quick as simply pushing a button, like it is on today's mountain bikes!

Once people have been mountain biking for a while, they usually decide it's worthwhile getting a few pieces of specialist equipment. This is aimed at making riding either more comfortable or safer.

Comfort Clothing

These are a few of the things people often buy to make mountain biking an extra bit more comfortable:

This rider is wearing typical clothing and equipment for a day out on the trail.

- Cycling tops with a long zipper at the front are good for letting out the heat during big uphill rides. Short-sleeved summer and long-sleeved winter versions are available.

- Cycling gloves, which have padding on the palms to stop your hands getting sore. These are available in long-fingered or short-fingered versions.

- Padded shorts can prevent soreness where your body touches the saddle. Choose from pants that go inside your ordinary shorts, clingy lycra tights with a built-in pad, or baggy shorts with a padded inner.

- A padded vest will add a little bit of extra warmth. A waterproof jacket is a good idea, too.

Safety Equipment

Downhill, 4X, and dual riders often wear body armor as protection, in case they fall off at high speed. This includes shin, knee, and arm pads, as well as **full-face helmets**. Sometimes they even wear armor on their **torso**, including a **spine protector**.

Accessories

Other gear includes special shoes and "clipless" pedals, backpacks with a section for carrying water, a tool kit, pump, spare inner tubes, and lights.

Downhill or "jump" gear: full-face helmet, goggles, and body armor.

Clipping In—and Out

Many top riders use clipless pedals. The pedal attaches to a cleat, a piece of metal screwed into the bottom of the rider's shoe. Learning to use clipless pedals can be quite tricky. If you topple over with both feet still attached, you won't be the first.

1 The cleat on the bottom of a special cycling shoe, which attaches to...

2 ... the clipless pedal.

3 Clip in by pushing the front of the cleat into the pedal, then pressing down. You will hear a little "click" as the pedal grips on.

4 To unclip, twist your foot sideways from the heel. Most people prefer to do this by twisting outward, but either way is fine.

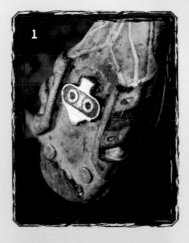

Basic Technique

Sports coaches sometimes say, "If you start right, you finish right." What they mean is that unless you start by learning basic techniques perfectly, it will be impossible to learn advanced ones. This is as true for mountain biking as it is for anything else.

"But everyone can ride a bike!"

Yes, almost everyone can— but not everyone rides a bike well. Some people use up a lot of energy without needing to. Just a little change to how you ride could make a big difference, and allow you to concentrate on enjoying the ride!

The two key elements of riding well are your position on the bike, and your pedaling speed. Your knees should be going pretty much straight up and down.

Aim to pedal smoothly, keeping your upper body as still and relaxed as possible. Ride with slightly bent arms.

Position on the Bike

The advice on page 8 will help you to reach a good basic riding position for XC and freeride. The seat height will allow you to use the powerful muscles in your legs and back for pedaling. The reach to the handlebars will give a fairly **aerodynamic** shape, but still make it easy to look at the trail ahead.

For downhill, 4X, and dual, mountain bikers set their seats lower and their handlebars higher. This gives them better control of the bike while going fast downhill.

Control your pedaling speed, or cadence, by using the gears.

A lower gear gives easier pedaling—good for going up hills.

A higher gear gives harder pedaling—good for downhill racing.

Cadence is Crucial

In cycling it is crucial to get your **cadence** (or pedaling speed) right. Too fast and you cannot get enough speed, and you will start bouncing in the saddle. Too slow will be tiring, and your riding technique will suffer. A good cadence to aim for is between 80 and 100 pedal strokes per minute. If you find it impossible to keep to this cadence, it means you are in the wrong gear.

The chain rings beside the pedals work in the opposite way from the freewheel. Here, the biggest cog is hardest and the smallest is the easiest.

The Uphill Grind

Most mountain bikers would probably say that riding uphill is the hardest, least favorite part of any ride. It doesn't have to be that way! Learning the following four techniques of uphill riding will have you whizzing up the slopes in a way that will astound your friends!

1 Get the Right Cadence

Picking the right gear is crucial for uphill riding, because if your cadence is too slow it makes the job much harder. Most riders like to spin the pedals a little faster than usual when they are riding uphill. That way, if the slope suddenly gets steeper you are ready for it. It's a good idea to start off in a slightly easier gear than you think you need.

2 Adjust Your Body Position

Slide back on the saddle, tuck in your elbows, and lean forward slightly to keep your weight over the front wheel. This allows your most powerful muscles to power you uphill, and keeps weight on both tires so they don't slip.

3 Stay Seated, Stay Still

Keep your upper body still, and stay seated on the saddle. Standing up burns energy very fast, and rocking your body from side to side will cause the bike to zigzag.

A good example of how to waste energy cycling uphill. The rider is standing on the pedals, pushing too hard a gear. He is waggling the handlebars from side to side, and his body and head are bobbing up and down.

This is good uphill technique. The rider has chosen a gear that allows him to spin the pedals, rather than every turn being a major effort. He has slid back on the saddle and is keeping his body still.

4 Pick a Clean Line

Try to follow a **line** (the path your tires take) that is free from mud, slippery tree roots, big rocks, or other things that could throw you off balance.

Uphill Racing

How's this for a challenge? The Purgatory Uphill Mountain Bike Race is held in Durango, Colorado. Here, racers ride almost 8 miles (13 km), climbing over 2,000 ft. (600 m) vertically up the mountainside!

Standing on the pedals for a short time can be used as a way of getting up a little speed for passing.

Downhill Rippers

Walk into a roomful of mountain bikers and ask who doesn't like riding downhill—not many will put their hands up. Unlike riding uphill, this is the part of mountain biking most people like best! But just like uphill riding, there are four tricks that can make your downhill technique faster, smoother, and safer:

1 Gear Selection

Cadence, or pedaling speed, is less important in downhill riding than in other kinds of mountain biking. This is just because you don't actually spend a lot of time pedaling. Even so, it is important to be in the right gear, so that you can accelerate whenever necessary. Pick a gear that will let you accelerate smoothly, without having to stand up on the pedals.

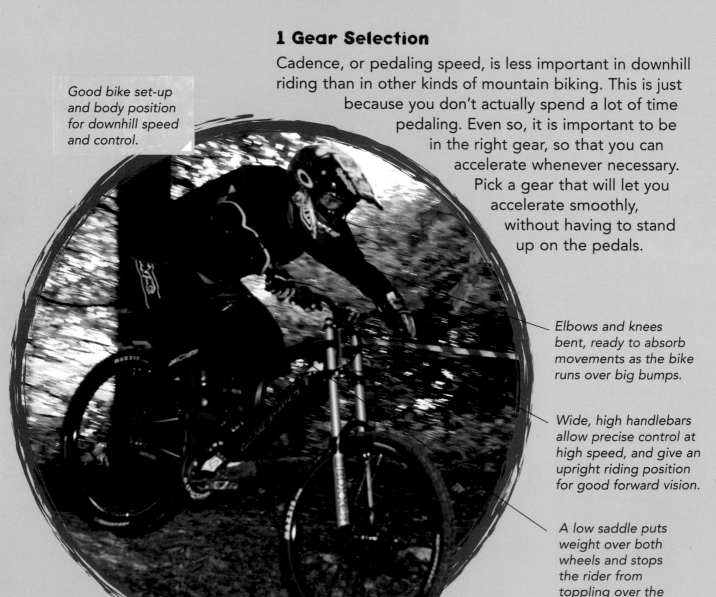

Good bike set-up and body position for downhill speed and control.

Elbows and knees bent, ready to absorb movements as the bike runs over big bumps.

Wide, high handlebars allow precise control at high speed, and give an upright riding position for good forward vision.

A low saddle puts weight over both wheels and stops the rider from toppling over the handlebars.

2 Body Position

Once the trail starts going downward, there is a danger of the rider leaning forward. This puts too much weight over the front wheel, which can lead to crashes or the rider toppling over the handlebars when the bike hits a bump. To stop this, riders put their saddle down lower than usual, and slide their weight backward. Some even hang their bottom out over the back wheel, resting their stomach on the saddle.

3 Look Ahead

Look ahead of you, down the trail. This is especially important when riding downhill, because big obstacles come up quickly! It's these big ones that could make you crash. The bike's tires and suspension will deal with small ones that you don't see until they are under your front wheel.

Anne-Caroline Chausson

Anne-Caroline Chausson is probably the best French mountain biker ever. Her list of achievements includes:

• Downhill world champion nine times.

• Dual world champion twice.

• 4X world champion twice.

• 2008 Olympic BMX champion.

Standing up on the pedals and bending his arms, this rider is ready to roll smoothly over obstacles. Notice how he is looking well ahead, down the slope.

4 Stay Loose

Try to stay relaxed on the bike. Most crashes happen when riders tense up and pull hard on the brakes, which makes the bike much less maneuverable.

Cornering Skills

When mountain bikers crash, it is often because they have come up to a corner too quickly. They pull hard on the brakes, and one of three things happens:

- The tires skid and they crash.
- The bike becomes hard to turn because the brakes are on, and they crash.
- They make it around the corner.

The Vanishing Point

There is a secret trick that will help make sure that the first two options never happen. It's called the vanishing point.

The vanishing point is the spot where you can see the two sides of a trail coming together. You can use it to judge how fast you should be going, and whether to speed up, slow down, or keep going at the same speed. It can be used in any kind of biking, or anything else where it's important to get your corner speed right: karting, motocross—even running!

Bend your inside elbow and stand up slightly on the pedals to give the tires a little extra grip while cornering.

Judging Your Speed

As you hurtle toward a corner, how can you judge whether you need to slow down, a lot, a little, or not at all? Do it like this:

1 Keep your vision fixed on the vanishing point. Is it moving closer to you? If so, you need to slow down.

2 If the vanishing point continues moving closer, brake harder.

3 Once the vanishing point is no longer moving toward you, you can stay at the same speed.

4 As the vanishing point moves away, start to accelerate again.

Keep looking ahead—don't be tempted to look down at the ground under your tires. You'll probably crash!

Keeping your weight forward while cornering will make the front tire less likely to slip on obstacles such as roots.

Body Position

Keeping your body in the right position will make your cornering smoother and faster:

• Stay seated or stand up very slightly on the pedals. Lean slightly forward so that there is weight over the front tire.

• Bend the elbow on the inside of the turn more than the one on the outside.

• Stretch your outside leg so that the pedal is as close to the ground as possible. This stops the inside pedal from catching on obstacles. Put weight on the outside pedal to give the tires an extra bit of grip.

Hazard Fixation

"Hazard fixation" is what experts call looking at what you're scared of. For example, you are riding and you see a big rock in the middle of the trail. You can't help looking at it—but try to look away! You will automatically steer the bike where you are looking. Stare at that rock, and you will probably hit it!

Riding Singletrack

Singletrack trails are so narrow that only one bike at a time can get down them. Whizzing along a thin track, zipping around obstacles with the trees and bushes brushing your elbows is a big thrill. Most mountain bike riders turn onto the singletrack whenever they can.

Types of Trail

The most popular type of singletrack is probably riding through woods. Zigging and zagging through the trees means the bike is hardly ever going in a straight line.

Many mountain-biking centers have purpose-built trails. Long sections of singletrack go along the slopes or downhill, while the riders quickly zip uphill on wide, smooth paths. The singletrack sometimes has specially banked turns and **ladders**. These are narrow, raised wooden pathways with a drop on each side. They test the rider's skill and nerve to the limit.

Low-hanging branches, slippery roots, rocks on the path, and other obstacles all make for an exciting singletrack ride.

Ride smoothly.

Stand on the pedals going downhill.

Ride a clean line.

Brake ahead.

Riding Tips

Singletrack riding is a big challenge for a rider's skills and reactions. There are a few tips that help make it flow more smoothly:

- Ride smoothly, without jerking your weight from side to side or forward and backward.

- Going downhill, stand up a little on the pedals and bend your elbows slightly, so that your legs and arms can absorb ups and downs.

- Ride a clean line. As far as possible, try to steer the bike along the smoothest route. Try to avoid riding over big roots and rocks, if possible.

- Brake ahead. Never brake while crossing a root or slippery rock, or you will skid.

- Use the vanishing point (see pages 20–21) to judge your cornering speed.

Riding Rooty Routes

Singletrack routes often go through woods, where the trails have roots growing across them. Roots are slippery and bike tires tend not to grip them well. When it's wet, they barely grip them at all.

The best way to ride across roots (and slippery rocks, too) is to go straight across them at an angle of 90 degrees. That way, if your tires slip, they are most likely to slip forward, which is the way you are going anyway.

Competition Mountain Biking

Most mountain bikers compete with their friends once in a while, seeing who can get up, down, or along a section of trail the fastest. For some riders, though, this isn't enough. They crave the thrill of serious racing. Fortunately, whatever level of skill, fitness, and experience you have, there is bound to be a race for you nearby.

Types of Competition

The main types of mountain bike race are XC, DH, 4X, and dual. There are lots of different levels of competition. The smallest contests are small, local races with just 40 or 50 riders. They take part for fun, or maybe to win a small trophy or a T-shirt.

There are also regional, national, and international championships, which are fought over by professional mountain bikers. The top level of competition is the **UCI** world series, which every year decides the best rider in each race discipline. Every four years, there is fierce competition to win Olympic gold in XC, the only mountain biking discipline at the Olympic Games.

Downhill racers get to the bottom as fast as possible, by riding, sliding, jumping—whatever is quickest!

12- and 24-Hour Racing

Among the most popular races on the mountain bike scene are 12- and 24-hour races. Solo riders, or teams of two or four, race around a course that is usually 3–6 miles (5–10 km) long. The winner is the rider who does the most laps within the time limit. The emphasis is on fun, with people camping by the course, DJs playing music, and food and beverages sold near the start and finish lines.

Riders setting out on a 24-hour race. The people taking it seriously make sure they start near the front. Those who are racing for fun are happy to be farther back.

During any race or ride lasting more than an hour, it is important to eat and drink regularly to keep your body fueled up.

Cyclocross

Cyclocross races are a little bit like mini 24-hour events. The riders complete a shorter course, usually for an hour, but sometimes the race is over a set distance instead. True cyclocross bikes have dropped handlebars and look like road-racing bikes with knobbly tires, but mountain bikes are usually allowed as well.

Race and Ride Better

Taking part in competitions improves your riding. For example:

- DH improves your mountain bike handling and cornering.

- XC improves your **endurance** (especially 24-hour XC racing).

- Dual and 4X improve your speed and **acceleration**.

25

Long-Haul Off-Roading

Most mountain bikers think a day in the saddle is a long ride. But there are some riders who think in terms of weeks, or even months, when they're planning a trip. These are the long-haul off-roaders.

Cycle Touring

Cycling is a great way to explore. Go by car and everything flies past too fast. Walk, and you don't get to see much because you can't cover much ground. But on a bike, you can cover a long distance each day, at a speed that allows you to see interesting places and enjoy the view. Traveling by bike in this way is called cycle touring.

When your family is selecting a camping spot, make sure you pick a sheltered, level area, away from overhanging trees.

Long-Haul Packing List

What to take for off-road touring depends on how long you are going for. Here are some simple guidelines to follow:

- **Always take:**

Food and beverages

Basic tool kit

Waterproof and warm clothes

Sleeping bag and mat

- **For one night**

Bivvy bag (a waterproof cover for your sleeping bag) or tent

Spare inner tube

- **For multiple nights**

Tent

Spare inner tubes, tire, and chain

Cooking equipment, plates, knife, and spoon

Two changes of clothes

When you are pedaling a long distance, you will need a lot of stuff—sometimes even a whole wheel's worth!

Off-Road Touring

Some touring cyclists prefer to stay off the beaten track. They go by off-road routes, enjoying the peace and safety of being away from the traffic. If this appeals to you, here are a few tips to get you started:

- Start small, perhaps with a one-night trip. This will give you a chance to figure out exactly what equipment you need.

- Decide how you are going to carry your gear. Backpacks are very uncomfortable on long rides. **Panniers** or a trailer are best.

- Practice packing before you go, to make sure everything fits. You can use any kind of XC bike for off-road touring. Most people use a fully rigid or hardtail bike. Simple bikes are better—you have to carry less spares, and they are easier to fix in the wilderness if something goes wrong!

Long-Distance Racing

A few mountain bikers have turned long-distance off-roading into a contest. These races are especially popular in North America. Examples include:

- The Iditarod: 1,120 miles (1,800 km) across the frozen wastes of Alaska, with no support crew, carrying all your own gear.

- The Great Divide Race: trail riding from Canada to Mexico on the Great Divide Mountain Bike Route. No support crew or other help allowed.

Biking Hot Spots

It doesn't matter where you live, you can mountain bike just about anywhere with access to off-road trails. But there's no doubt some mountain biking locations are better than others. If you could go anywhere in the world, no expense spared, where would your dream ticket take you? Some, at least, of the following would have to be on the list:

Biking in the UK

Some of the UK's best trails are in Wales. In the south, purpose-built mountain bike centers provide exhilarating riding. In the north, purpose-built trails combine with other great routes you can find for yourself.

In Scotland, the main biking attraction is the "7 Stanes." This is a group of seven mountain bike locations with thrilling trails, some **lift-assisted**. The most famous is Fort William, at the foot of Ben Nevis, the UK's highest mountain.

Spectacular singletrack trails, beautiful mountain rides, and the opportunity for some fun. Wales has a lot to offer the mountain biker!

Biking in the U.S.A.

The United States has a good claim to being the birthplace of mountain biking. It is still home to some of the world's best biking, including:

- Northern California, particularly around Marin County, north of San Francisco. The woods and hills of Marin County are one of the places where mountain biking first became popular.

- The East Coast, particularly in and around Vermont. Here, many ski resorts keep their lifts open in the summer for use by riders.

- Moab, Utah, which has an amazing variety of trails through an eerie, rocky landscape.

Biking in Europe

There are numerous popular mountain bike areas across mainland Europe. Ski resorts in Scandinavia, the Alps, the Dolomites, and the Pyrenees all allow riders to take their bikes up the mountain using lifts, then come racing back down on specially designed routes. Some of the top spots include Morzine-Les Gets in the French Alps, Vallnord in Andorra, and Hafjell in Norway.

Biking in Australia and New Zealand

In Australia, two of the best mountain biking areas are the Blue Mountains, west of Sydney, and the Snowy Mountains in the state of northern Victoria.

In New Zealand, thrill-seekers of all kinds flock to Queenstown on the shores of Lake Wakatipu. One of the big attractions is heli-biking. A helicopter takes you and the bike to the top of a route no one else can reach, and you get to ride it all the way back down, alone.

The moonlike landscape of the desert near Moab, Utah, has been a favorite with mountain bikers for years.

Have Bike, Will Travel

If you want to go biking in a foreign country, you might decide to take your bike with you. Most airlines carry bikes (they usually make a charge), though taking a bike on the train can be tricky.

Otherwise, you could rent a bike when you get there. Booking in advance on the Internet ensures you get the bike you want.

Glossary

Acceleration This means to increase in speed.

Aerodynamic The ability to slip easily through the air.

Bottom bracket The part of a bike frame to which the cranks are attached.

Cadence The speed of pedaling. Pedaling fast is called having a high cadence; pedaling slowly, a low cadence.

Coaster brake This is a brake hidden inside the hub of the back wheel, which comes on when the rider pedals backward.

Cranks The metal arms to which the pedals are attached.

Derailleurs A device that makes a bicycle change gear.

DH This is short for downhill, a style of mountain biking.

Disc brakes These are brakes that work by gripping onto a disc of metal, which is attached to the wheel axle.

Endurance The ability to do something for a long time.

Fork This is the part of the bike that the front wheel attaches to.

Full speed The highest possible speed you can ride.

Full-face helmets A helmet with a section that comes down around the face and in front of the chin.

Headset These are hidden sets of ball bearings at the front of the frame, which allow the forks to be turned smoothly from side to side.

Ladders These are narrow, raised wooden pathways with a drop on each side.

Lift-assisted This means using a ski lift to climb uphill.

Line This refers to the path that your tires take.

Panniers These are bags that attach to a rack on the bike, and hang down beside the wheel. The most common panniers hang beside the rear wheel.

Play This refers to looseness or movement in a mechanism.

Pressure gauge A device for checking the air pressure in a tire. Some pumps have a built-in pressure gauge. The pressure is measured in units called psi.

Resistance The force that slows or stops movement. At speeds of over about 9 mph (15 km/h), air resistance slows down cyclists.

Rim brakes These are bicycle brakes that work by pushing a rubber pad against each rim of the wheel.

Spine protector A set of reinforced or padded plates that are designed to protect the spine in a crash.

Suspension A system of springs that is designed to absorb the shocks caused by traveling over rough or uneven ground.

Top tube The uppermost bike frame tube, running between the handlebars and the rear of the bike.

Torso The trunk of the body. The part that your neck, arms, and legs are all attached to.

Travel This means "movement." In cycling, the amount that a bike's suspension moves is called its travel.

True This means "straight."

UCI Union Cycliste Internationale, or International Cycling Union, the world governing body for cycle sports.

XC This is short for cross-country, a style of mountain biking.

Further Reading and Web Sites

Books to Read

BMX and Mountain Biking: The World's Best Parks, Trails, Streets, and Techniques
by Paul Mason
(Capstone Press, 2010)

Mastering Mountain Bike Skills
by Brian Lopes
(Human Kinetics, 2010)

Mountain Biking
by Hollie Edres
(Children's Press, 2007)

Zinn and the Art of Mountain Bike Maintenance
by Lennard Zinn
(VeloPress, 2005)

Web Sites

Due to the changing nature of Internet links, PowerKids Press has developed an online list of Web sites related to the subject of this book. This site is updated regularly. Please use this link to access this list:
http://www.powerkidslinks.com/go/mount

index